THE SIGN OF THE CROW

THE SIGN OF THE CROW

poems by

Ignacio Ruiz-Pérez

translated by

Carlos Reyes

Lynx House Press
Spokane, Washington

ACKNOWLEDGMENTS

Some of these poems first appeared in the following publications:

Askew, Hubbub & Salt River Review

The Sign of the Crow was originally published as *Navegaciones* (Gobierno de Chiapas, 2006). In 2005 the volume was awarded the Rodulfo Figueroa Regional Poetry Prize (Mexico).

Copyright © 2011 Carlos Reyes

Printed in America.

Cover art: "The King of Bing" by Melissa Cole
Author photo: Luisa Ruiz
Cover & book design: Christine Holbert

FIRST EDITION

Library of Congress Cataloging-in-Publication Data

Ruiz Pérez, Ignacio, 1976-
[Navegaciones. English]
The sign of the crow: poems / by Ignacio Ruiz-Pérez; translated [from the Spanish] by Carlos Reyes.—1st ed.
     p. cm.
Originally published as Navegaciones in 2006.
ISBN 978-0-89924-122-7 (alk. paper)
1. Ruiz Pérez, Ignacio, 1976—Translations into English. I. Reyes, Carlos, 1976- II. Title.
PQ7298.428.U455N3813 2011
861'.7—dc22
                    2011009713

CONTENTS

ASYMMETRIES

THE SIGN OF THE CROW

VOYAGES

To Ignacio Ruiz Rasgado,
Elsiaria Pérez Castro, Ana Luisa Ruiz Pérez and Ilya Cortés Ruiz

For Alicia

ASYMMETRIES

ELEGY ON THE DEATH OF WILLIAM BLAKE

William Blake:
nocturnal is the bird that perched on you
to burn its plumage
in your song of an old pirate.

Without knowing
you put in your logbook
the silhouette of gulls
the rhythm of waves
and nights foretold.

Nothing draws me to you
like the solitude of your immense skull
and your eyes like a summer
of brightest suns.

William Blake:
may the night write your epitaph.

CARNIVAL IN CHAMULA

The flags, the pine masks,
the hard lines of dreams: total inebriation,
total light, an impulse that begins with life
and ends with life, a dawn of the thickest
beauty because in its transparent brilliance
the sum total of destiny resides, movement
of the stars, and heaven's writing.

CESARE PAVESE, THE SEA
AND TWO DRAGONFLIES

for Maricarmen Acedo and José María Rueda

According to what you say, a gram

of energy equals two days

at the sea you never knew,

but fatigue—

how can it be measured?

Could it be that skin stretched out beneath the sun

is not twice as ephemeral

and pure as thirst or a photograph?

Two dragonflies pair up

and everything comes to an end—

the waters flow

toward the same channel

and even though there is nothing

that disintegrates twice,

the arm that has fallen asleep

collapses and results

always

in the same look.

SELF-PORTRAIT OF COLERIDGE

He draws his raw face:

a sepia image

and the curved line of his nose.

The wickedness that changes

dawn strips his

thoughts bare.

He sketches a smile:

a pair of gulls,

three bearded fish,

and an old sailor

sink slowly into his eyes.

FACES

While patients in clinics
meditate
on the mercury in thermometers
Pascal thinks of the flame
the Bunsen burner spits out:
a single flame and its duration
reminds us of barking dogs
when they crowd up against a wall
or rub against each other.
Pascal asks himself: Could it be
this flame is the apex of certainty
that incinerates God, science, and art?
Or is it the persistence of death
that verifies
the punctuality of oblivion?
When Pascal reaches out with his hand
to the flame he proves
the existence of the world.

BILLY BUDD ENCHAINED

There is nothing left but travel

see the deserted islands

weigh anchor

listen to songs of the sirens

tie myself to the mast

and scan the sea to the south . . .

The passage of time doesn't frighten me:

the gasping fish tied to starboard

scares me more.

Looking at its teeth,

I think of the morning: opening

beneath the lens of a microscope,

approaching the poisonous frogs

that will likely be put

on my tongue

to keep me from speaking

the language of the waves.

DUSK IN ALFAMA

The young fado singer
contemplates the terraces
surrounding the castle
of San Jorge
her thought
a flight of birds
a zig-zag
describing a circle
around her hunched-over body.
Beyond that, nothing:
not even the view that holds
what approaches
at bay.

At his passing, bridges

stop the hours,

Big Ben is a suspended

period,

Virginia Woolf contemplates

a shop window

and a ship hastens its

return to Ithaca.

Is there anything else to remember?

You carry it all in your memory,

even daybreak

that enters through the door

and leaves through the window.

GREGORIO DE MATOS
WRITES FROM HIS DEATHBED

for Daniel Aguilar, Nelly Barrientos, Rodolfo Mendoza, and Manuel Licea

I don't write: I think in syllables

composed by the night.

I don't think: I resort to the indecipherable

mirror of dawn.

On both shores my night blindness

lights up the poem and then

lances, horses, and the tower

recoup their limits in the abacus

that counts the hours of exile.

I have died many times:

at the Battle of Lepanto,

in the circular corridors

of the Convent of Carmine,

in the eyes reflected in the dagger,

and in the shot from the harquebus.

I have lived in all the names

and all the names have had my face.

Today nothing of me remains.

Only this line that changes into

dust and emptiness.

THE TIGER IN ITS LABYRINTH

for Almudena Cabezas and Brett Joly, twenty years later

They have left behind hours and days.

They have left behind the city and its mirrors.

In the markets the shopkeepers sell

the bundle of its shadow and shroud of Christ,

the story of amounting to little, of being nobody or nothing.

From my house which grows with the day

and diminishes with the night,

I hear murmurs in the plaza.

Serpents coil themselves around the neck of a contortionist

and an Arab crosses his body with the vowels of the Sacred Book.

From my house I hear the tongues of pilgrims,

and I, the same as them, am Babel,

the thirst of the camel in the dunes impossible to imagine,

and the reflection of the sun in the depths of the well.

In the endless days I am able to cross the walls

that surround my terrestrial condition.

In the nights, by contrast, I remain tied

to the bars that destiny has imposed.

I am tired. Nobody—not even me—is interested

in this time passing, this dream, this agony.

THE SIGN OF THE CROW

THE SIGN OF THE CROW

Crows swear that a single crow can destroy the heavens.
Doubtlessly, this is true, but the fact doesn't prove anything to the heavens,
because the heavens signify nothing except the impossibility of crows.

—*Franz Kafka*

A great flight of crows stains the celestial blue.

—*Rubén Darío*

for Jorge Brash

1

When I got to the city the sky was a murmur of wings.

Squawking broke the skin of the world,

their faces crackling, broken ribs, shoots of water,

a reflection buried itself like a knife in the dungeons of the afternoon,

their cloudy presence posed a question,

a blow, a peck, claws weakened the walls,

a murmur of wings blackened time,

the birds appeared between gaps in the water

sinking into it their blue beaks and metallic feathers,

their claws tore off dark skin and scarcely left holes

where something like eternity appeared,

their feathers sprinkled the world's silence,

their eyes looked for eyes; images fallen, broken

and opened like skulls displaced by infinity.

Now and then the trees presented themselves as signs

alive with dark birds, like days of fever.

One bird with a broken head awaited the final blow.

2

Then it was night:

the tallest oak covered itself with shadows,

caws were branches hanging from the dawn.

"They have pulled out my eyes," accused an old man

leaning on a stone wall.

"Now they feed on the stomach of the night,"

someone younger pointed out while the drainpipes of the church

and the clock of the evening stood out against the buildings.

"My eyes are a nest of starlings,"

pronounced a man with a pallid look and an empty face.

3

A shattered scream, open like the palm of a hand
where the most absolute lines of silence cross,
a cry that turns and slips into the depths of the sea,
its immense falling, its body broken,
entrails like tiny flowers
that sprout from the eyes of morning.

4

(Round)

one, two, three: he's one-eyed
has a face and doesn't see

in the tiger's house
the children throw dice
he's one eyed: one, two, three:
they walk two by two
with closed lips
He has a face and doesn't see

the youngest skips rope
smiles with bandaged eyes
. . . the one-eyed man is king

5

Their eyes caught fire

tense

      vibrant

their eyes were light,

and the gold of day ashes,

the sea divided:

four pillars kept up a conversation

with horses of luminous manes,

a lightning bolt separated the lovers,

turning them to dust and scattering their remains,

water opened their thighs

and night penetrated their smooth skin.

The earth opened and spat up snakes

that wrapped themselves around the throat of time.

And this was what happened:

they strangled it, they exploded its veins,

impregnating its round belly with words.

Some crows flew into the branches of night,

scaling the notes of the moon, tore out the eyes of time

and squawked until dawn.

6

Forces of fate or embers of night,

the crows reflect the world in their eyes.

That's why they believe they keep watch over others

when really they only watch out for themselves.

Appetite devours them daily,

so let them feed on the reflections they encounter

among the discards of the afternoon.

7

People often confuse them with barriers and reefs
because their squawking, a gathering of laments that epitomize
their skin and hungry eyes, wrecks ships and brings down trees.
When they walk they imitate the falling leaves
blown along in a quiet kind of penitence
their hairy feet trace signs and a coat of arms.

8

They open their wings to cover their solitude and seek in their chests
a fistful of signs; they rough up their feathers,
fight for a scrap of wood or an old bottle,
they rummage around in the glance of their neighbor for their own look
and settle down in the branches to think in the twilight.

9

If the sea breeze doesn't carry them away it's because a tenacity
akin to anguish keeps them tied to the trees.
The pounding of the sea frightens them.
Then the branches creak and the silence is more
like the night and the crows more like the void:
a pyre of eyes staring down at death.

10

When they get old their feet curve like their beaks

and wings become a reflection of one another,

the left wing slightly more symmetrical

because the right wing is pulled out of its track

and a bit more injured,

because the sun shone fully on the left.

They hop, achieve half flight;

they know there is no loss greater

than being the reflection of themselves,

nor any gain smaller than ending up

with their glower turned into uncut stones.

11

Then it was night:
the branches creaked,
their beaks tore into the bellies of the trees
and a thousand crows were launched to devour
hundreds of ants, four dragonflies
and a robin.

12

(Round)

eye, knife, and sword:
colt of water, flaming mane

afternoon devours the day,
a meeting, and a crossroads
eye, knife, and sword

night engulfs the afternoon
after sunrise
colt of water, flaming mane

under the half moon
the horseman wakes in a coffin
. . . sees nothing

VOYAGES

And you don't talk. Don't talk,
since you no longer speak in riddles
perhaps I have lost you by knowing you.

—*Gilberto Owen*

IN THE SHADOW OF THE DAY

I

The Wanderer observes the curve of water.

Return is not possible: only the aroma of stranded boats

and darkness that winks in the remnants of the afternoon.

And in the anchorages the cries of men break through the distance:

the setting sun nods along the shores of a vastness that raises my glance,

the horizon tunes its ears to trap the days

of insomnia and desperation,

and the world is a silent cavity, an empty hope,

a call without answer.

Beyond, the sun reflects the Wanderer's look

while the lines crackle in the austere loneliness of block and tackle.

II

I measure the intensity of the sunset: a garden of jasmine is crowded into the depths of the water. Crabs chew the hair of the drowned, their eyes purple with the gradations of light, clothing hangs in currents subterranean and transparent as a boy's smile. I walk aimlessly, guided by memory that rescues me at every moment and that at every moment disappears. On the dock the travelers say goodbye to their families as though they were saying goodbye to themselves and the waters set aflame the limestone sheds, the carved walls of the temples where the tide arrives like a sign raised up in the hands of a girl.

III

Behold the intentions of the sea:

the surface whips the keels of the ships,

the world opens up to the night,

the albatross takes flight like an *idée fixe,*

salt devours the flames of torches and cargo ships

anchored to chains smelling of rust,

a merchant uncovers bags of sapphires and lapis lazuli,

a squeaking of metals beheads the traces of sunset

while a crowd watches the removal

of cadavers hurled toward the questioning night.

IV

On the isle of Levant there is a hamlet that spreads up the transparent slopes of a mountain. Its white streets are trapped in the light of day and its houses have tiny canopies that serve as shelter from the rain. Its inhabitants stop to listen to music: stagnant notes from the ditch of the afternoon and doves picking at the barest light that falls through tree branches among the cupolas of the churches. Children entertain themselves with portions of forgetfulness that hang from the almond trees like leaves, while women go out with wicker baskets in which they keep love like white questions. The men contemplate the ceiba trees: the soft roots breaking the teeth of the dead into fine pieces, and branches like wings or handkerchiefs. With their harmonicas old men intone ancient songs that slide through the smoke of the ovens where the women burn a disorderly silence. When the bells clang, the people sleep and dream about a village of white streets spread out along the transparent slopes of a mountain.

V

May your head be removed from your body,

may your memory be the tomb of your presence,

may your morning be the profile of solitude

and rubbish of your earthly condition,

may humidity and niter enter your eyes

and dispose of the last images of day,

may tar fall upon your lineage and salt impregnate your exile,

may your word be erased from the mouth of man,

may your tongue and your name be dust.

VI

In the presence of air
a cry bursts into flames

The sea is coming with its winged reflection

The echo hangs its shadow
burning the strings of the wind

The sea is coming with its winged reflection

Memory falls from the chopping block
With that blow the afternoon comes to a close

The sea is coming with its winged reflection

VII

The roof tiles absorb the relentless sound of water:

its song, swollen with rumors

and prophecies, rocks the embers of afternoon,

the sap that flows from dead wood, smelling of mahogany,

when the pounding rain covers

the quiet face of desire with mud

and a man runs to get out of the rain

as if he were running to meet his death.

VIII

Sometimes I remember the thin line that divides the expression of the sea,

the sound of shorelines, water as an invention of forgetfulness,

a gesture of the infinite or a painful farewell.

Then the north wind licks our faces,

nets hang from the windows of houses,

and ropes tie together the remains of reeds

like gestures that crown lost undertakings.

IX

This is the route that the Wanderer followed one feverish night:

The prow searches for the shores indicated by the sextant,

the trajectory of gulls falls on the horizon

like a pile of rotten logs,

keels screech from the battering of heavy seas,

a port found in the middle of a dream

hides its houses of stone,

later there is the trace of morning on the island of Levant,

the harvest of spices and cargos of silk,

the murmur of markets where the seasons hold

pelicans flapping their wings, the odor of fish and cries of children,

then the sailors' songs announcing the end of the day,

girls that uncover breasts redolent of sandalwood,

rocks that devour the flight of gulls,

the indecisive look of lovers,

their bodies naked and warm, recently opened up to desire,

finally the mangrove swamps, the roots,

transparent bays,

the houses a foreshadowing of what will come

and the woods, the ceiba trees afire with warm currents,

the fine sand of the rivers that cross the port

and flow out into the sea like a fish

accepting the nearness of death,

the naves of churches where oblivion waits
to drink the geography of Ariadne,
a body that has known love
and has run away to the provinces of dawn.

X

The port of Ariadne rises along the shores of the sea like a thought. The traders tie up their ships during the day and unload boxes and bundles that look like eyes popped out between the rotten planking. Sailors walk around the white houses as if searching for the reflection of the afternoon. Fish move through the blue waters like the hands of the dead and fasten themselves to the swollen prows of ships: their fins hold back the water's movement and their scales capture the dead waves, the currents in which seaweed seems like miniscule fragments of light.

There are no waters more precise than those of the port of Ariadne: the tide covers the city by night and by day leaves it intact, clean, like the breast of an albatross. The sea loses its tints and hues: he who looks for the port at night will find himself in the middle of a mound of shadows, and echoes that scarcely give an idea of the city's shape.

During the day, the streets surround themselves with reflections of the sun, giving them the appearance of another more ethereal Ariadne. In the plaza the albatross trace smooth trajectories against the intense light of the sun that descends through the palm-thatched roofs. Then the gardens become more numerous as the walkers pass from one reflection to another and the sea multiplies, like memory.

XI

Ah, my splendid one, I have come to you wounded and ready to cross the swamp

that surrounds the bulwarks, the thick limestone walls,

the streets of the villages resplendent in reflected sunlight,

and the large vineyards that fill the countryside.

Next to the sea, the first gulls draw a circle around the morning

as ships leave to find the rhythm of the waves, trading, and spices.

To you—who doubtless are the wall, the mantle

and the wasted face of the name, the splendor of the moon for the hanged man,

and the sentence for the suicide—

the waves arrive to undress the fruits of the sea, the heavy mist in the West,

anchors that hold back the breathing of the dead, the head of hair spread out

on the dissection table, and the promises inhabited by oblivion.

May age never surprise your eyes, may salt never touch your hands,

nor the rumor of the breeze inflame your thinking in the solitude of death.

XII

I come down to listen to the cries of pelicans

that accompany the arrival of ships.

A sailor lets go the anchors,

another notices his absence in the depth of a telescope.

The sails come down like the afternoon

announcing the arrival of the north wind

and a boat rocks

with the cries of seagulls

when they drop down to peck at the remains of a dog

floating in the water.

XIII

Next some of the Wanderer's most precious objects turn up:

a map eaten by the worms of fever,

a logbook of his most terrible acts of madness,

a rusted telescope, a crucifix,

some gold coins that shine like the eyes of the dead,

a cord covered with the white salt of ominous hours,

a bit of a ballad heard from a virgin's lips,

a handkerchief with an inscription in an exotic language,

a saber, a book, and a parchment.

XIV

The afternoon falls like lead over the tanned hides,
over roof tiles where some curlews perch,
waiting for the remnants of guts or questions
that the sailors will throw like harpoons.
A small razor cuts a slice of thought
and perplexity falls between the planks on the dock
like a sack thrown into the water.
And later, the signs of night: the phrases never mentioned,
the beginning of the hours fighting against darkness
while a ship runs aground in the sleeping light
and eyes shape my memories.

XV

The city of Alba is spread out like arms around a bay shaped like a young woman's hips. Its white houses seem to swing back and forth when the north winds or those from the south sweep the dusty streets, the plazas surrounded by fire ant trees like defeated sentinels watching over the disorder of the world. At dawn the old fishermen drag in nets that will sink in the sea like ancient litanies.

Once on the high sea, the fishermen stop to listen to the moan of the water, the song of unknown women, wet planks of the hull plowing through the waves. Then the horizon is filled with quiet aromas and cries that come from sadness. The edge of the sea buries itself in the throat of the air, a gull follows in arced flight the wake of the ferries. The fishermen look toward shore where kitchen smoke waves goodbye sadly, and in silence they watch the dock, the arrival of galleons, and their smooth contact with the bollards where they will be tied up for a century or two.

In the middle of the afternoon, the city of Alba looks like a smiling boy.

XVI

The last scream of the gulls falls as if it were diving on prey.
The Wanderer mumbles a few words, raises his hands toward the mast
where a piece of white cloth catches the reflections
    of the empty afternoon
over the heads of the drunks who have come out to acknowledge
    their deaths.
And here are their thoughts on that afternoon of fallen wings
    and bitter phrases:
the train tracks are lost in my memory,
some beggars hold out their hats to trap
the reflections of the hours lost in the bottles of rum,
and smoke from the houses mixes with the slap
of the rowers' oars during fishing season.
Sometimes I hear a single cry that buries itself
in the waters and the directionless days.
Then I can decipher the signs of tedium,
the rottenness of the wood
on the point of crushing the succession of hours,
and the words that try to establish the idea of oblivion.

You will see how they will dismember and incinerate your body in the fire of day.

·

Your hair will fall out, your teeth will roll on the ground, and your grimacing face will be weathered and tanned by the north wind.

·

You will see the ships dip their clumsy hands in the waters so there be will no living form left on the face of the earth that doesn't seek its reflection in the foam.

·

The stones will be ripped from the roofs of houses and strike the bellies of those who sit in the house of man.

·

The furrows of the earth will bring forth two-headed serpents that will fill the tongues of men with confusion.

·

The tree will fill with curlews and wormy fruits. And the young men of earth will take shade beneath the almond trees and eat the bitterest of seeds.

·

And the shadows of men will follow their owners through plazas and streets until they absorb the presence of the world.

·

Silence will penetrate the bones of the shadows until their skins burst. And in man's refuge no stone will remain standing.

•

And men will stare through telescopes and see only flies and buzzards swarming over the bones of their children.

•

SCATTERED JOTTINGS OF THE WANDERER

(Entries from the Log Book)

First Day

Then we saw the islands.

Days earlier we spotted gulls circling,

cormorants throwing themselves with all their might against the waves,

the scales of some of the fish reflecting

remnants of nights past.

The teeth of some of the sailors rotted from scurvy.

Second Day

We loosened the lines and furled the sails.
The sea surrounded us with the aroma of orange blossoms.
The port of swollen dock planks rose in the background
and at the foot of a village, a mountain covered with crosses
crowned the sky.

Third Day

The dead are so many that the cemetery
looks like a city of small cathedrals.
The houses have patios and in the center
there almost always are medlar trees.
The fruits of this country are transparent
and their nectar of a substance like silence.
The people customarily rake up seeds
from the roads, the gardens, the closed patios,
and the cement sidewalks to guarantee the permanence
of silence. Each tree planted, they say, assures them of oblivion.
And so the old ones go out to discover
the shadow's angle which coincides with
their hour of death.

Fourth Day

The women stay home
and only go out to sell or buy flowers,
fish, and things needed around the house.
The men stay in bed, cradling death,
putting off the thought of winter.
The children gather around the medlar tree,
pick the fruit, and bring it to their lips
as though they were stammering out a song.

Fifth Day

Here solitude is so great that the houses
have sheds to protect them from it.
A series of chutes crosses the roofs
that end in gargoyles in the form of fishes,
and large vineyards branch out endlessly:
a hand appears between the leaves and the grapes,
a pair of wings, bats, tiny teeth,
limestone decorations, angels that battle dawn
with fallen wings, dragons that set fire
to space, ceaseless blows, a family tree
of fishes and whales with chunks of amber
encrusted in their bodies, always
accompanied by shrimp and mollusks:
a concert of organic material
and birds that cross the myriad
dimensions of the walls.

Sixth Day

Today I have seen amber mines shining in the sun.
I have seen muleskinners searching the south quadrant of the horizon.
I have seen faces, backs burned,
feet splintered, souls in fragments
like the months and seasons.
I have seen the fruits of the world,
the horizon devouring the light of autumn,
the seagulls crossing the sky.
I have seen everything, and that's enough.

Seventh Day

Farther on are the temples, the streets,
the proclamations in the plaza, the clay sheds
where night hides out.

From the other side of the sea they execute a man,
someone testifies in favor of dishonor,
the assassin buries a dagger in the back of his brother,
the Pharisee makes three gold doubloons ring,
the slanderer yanks out the tongue from his adversary,
young women go to the park with baskets
of fruit, without yet knowing love or sadness.

Even farther beyond, my eyes watch the passing of birds,
the noise of prows opening the way
through deserted waters.
Ahead of me the city and the dock,
the fences and bridges multiply.
I cross the first planks:
my past is a succession of dead moments.
I keep going: farther along are the church,
the arches, altarpieces, ballustrades.
I turn and watch my image:
from this side I see myself as he who was;
from the other, he who will be.
I continue to exist.

ABOUT THE TRANSLATOR

CARLOS REYES is a noted poet and translator. His most recent volume is *The Book of Shadows; New and Selected Poems* (2009). Other recent titles include: *At the Edge of the Western Wave* (2004) and *A Suitcase Full of Crows* (1995). His books of translations include *Poemas de la Isla/ Island Poems* by Josefina de la Torre (Eastern Washington University Press, 2000) and *Obra poética completa (Complete Poetic Works)* of the preeminent Ecuadorean poet Jorge Carrera Andrade, published in 2004 in a bilingual edition in Ecuador. He is the publisher/editor of Trask House Books, Inc., and has been a fellow at the Fundación Valparaíso in Mojácar, Spain, and at Yaddo. In 2007 he was awarded a Heinrich Boll Fellowship on Achill Island, Ireland. He was recently the poet-in-Residence in the Joshua Tree National Park. Reyes lives in Portland but travels often to Ireland and is a frequent visitor also to Spain and Ecuador.